MOUSE!

By Carrie Hyatt
Illustrated by Sandra Figueras

DEDICATION

This story is dedicated to everyone who desires to overcome the debilitating affects of fear. Sometimes, when fear gets in the way, we can't see what is really in front of us.

GET READY TO SHOUT, "**MOUSE!**"
WITH EACH OPPORTUNITY IN THE STORY.

ONE DAY, WITHOUT A CLOUD IN VIEW, THE SKY GREW VERY DARK. A SHADOW COVERED THE EARTH LIKE A BLANKET AS THE MOON PASSED IN FRONT OF THE SUN.

WHILE EVERYONE ELSE
ADJUSTED TO THE DARKNESS,

ONE WOMAN
CLOSED
HER EYES FOR
A SHORT NAP.

THIS WAS HIS CHANCE. A MOUSE BOLDLY RACED OUT TO EXPLORE HER HOUSE.

TO HIS SURPRISE,
THERE WAS PLENTY
TO EAT EVERYWHERE!

CELEBRATING

30

NIGHTTIME ANIMALS BECOME ACTIVE DURING A SOLAR ECLIPSE!

AS THE TIME TICK, TICK, TICKED BY, THE DARKNESS BEGAN TO PEEL AWAY FROM THE HOUSE. WITHIN A FEW MINUTES, THE SUN PEEKED OUT AGAIN.

THE MOUSE PULLED HIS HEAD OUT OF A CUPCAKE, AND THE LIGHT CAUGHT THE CRUMBS THAT FELL FROM HIS CHEEKS.

THE WOMAN YAWNED.

"OH, NO!" SQUEALED THE MOUSE, AND THE WOMAN OF THE HOUSE HEARD HIM!

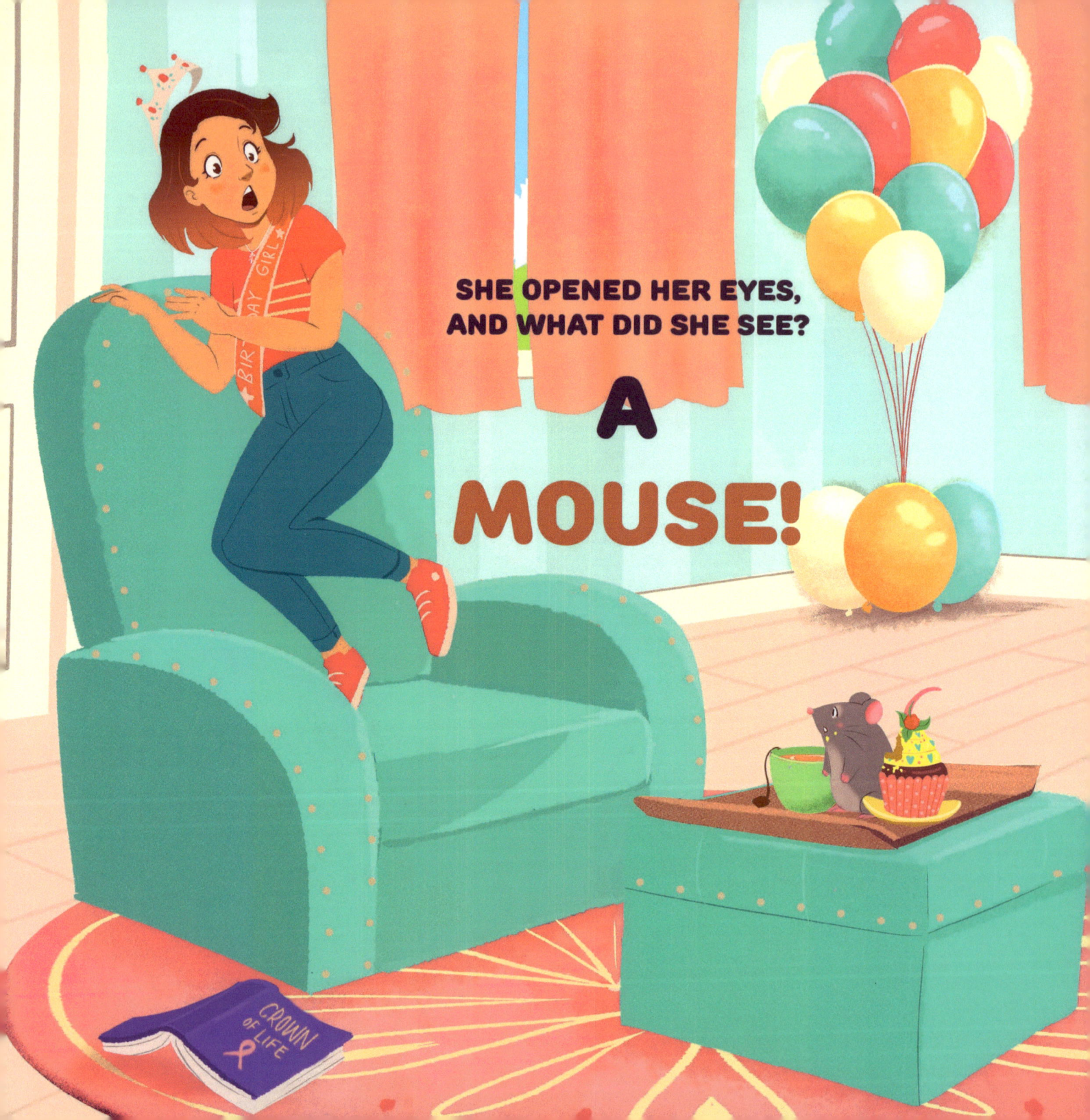

SHE OPENED HER EYES,
AND WHAT DID SHE SEE?

A
MOUSE!

THAT'S RIGHT. SO WHAT DID SHE SCREAM WITH ALL OF HER MIGHT?

"MOUSE!"

THE LITTLE MOUSE FROZE. HE DIDN'T DARE MOVE.
HE WAS SCARED AS HE STARED AT THE WOMAN OF THE HOUSE.

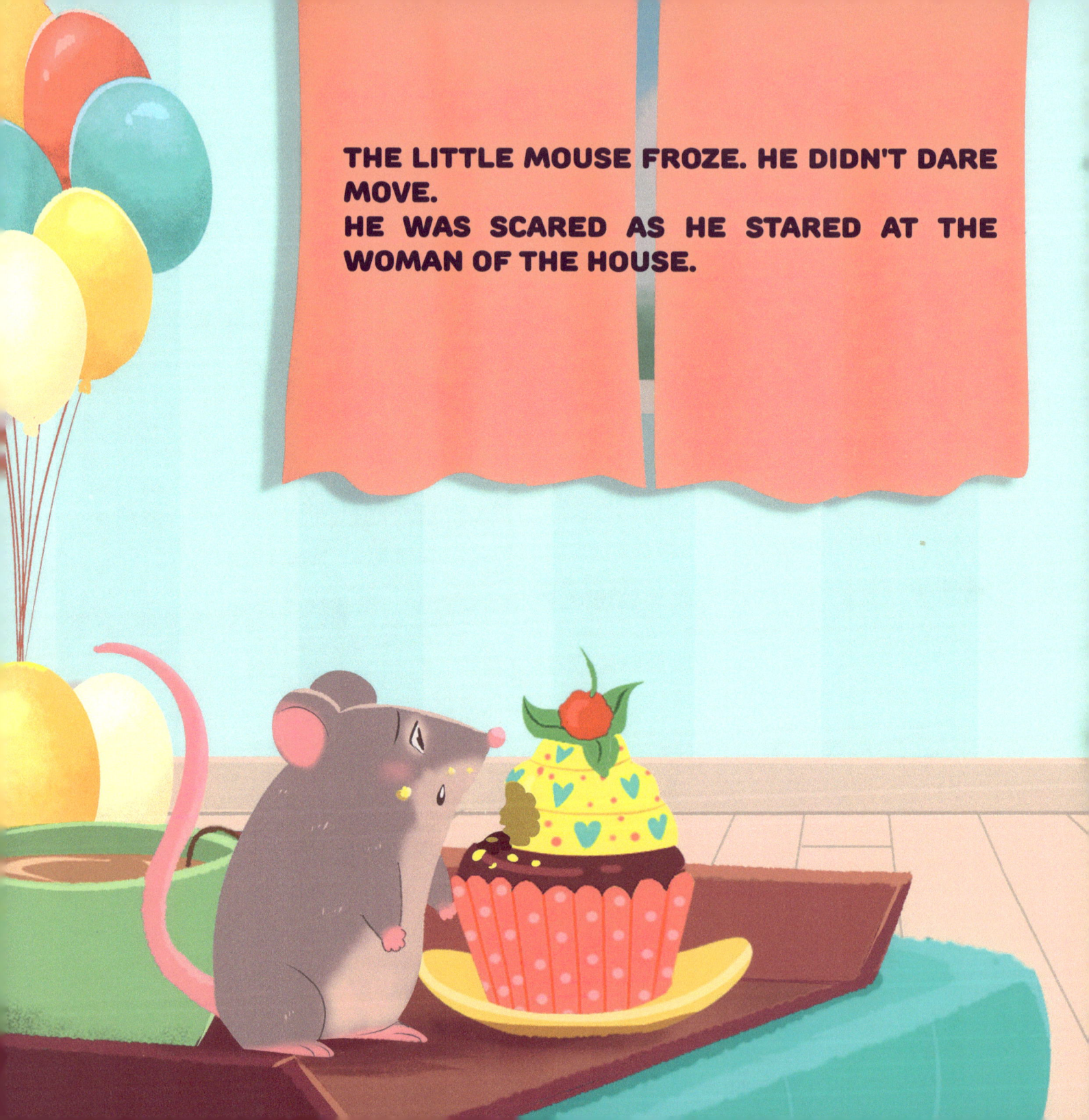

THE WOMAN STARED BACK. SHE DIDN'T MOVE EITHER.

A MOSQUITO LANDED ON THE WOMAN'S NOSE. SHE CRINGED BUT HELD THE MOUSE'S GLARE.

A FLEA BIT THE MOUSE'S LEG. OH! HOW IT PRICKED HIM, BUT THE MOUSE DIDN'T FLINCH.

A SOUND BEEPED FROM THE OVEN, BUT THE WOMAN OF THE HOUSE IGNORED THE TIMER.

BEEP BEEP!!!

A CAT WRIGGLED ITS BOTTOM, READY TO POUNCE. THE MOUSE THOUGHT, I'M A GONER! BUT THE CAT JUMPED ON THE CURTAINS.

HER EYES BURNED.
HER NOSE ITCHED.
WITH ONE MORE CRY SHE YELLED,

"MOUSE!"

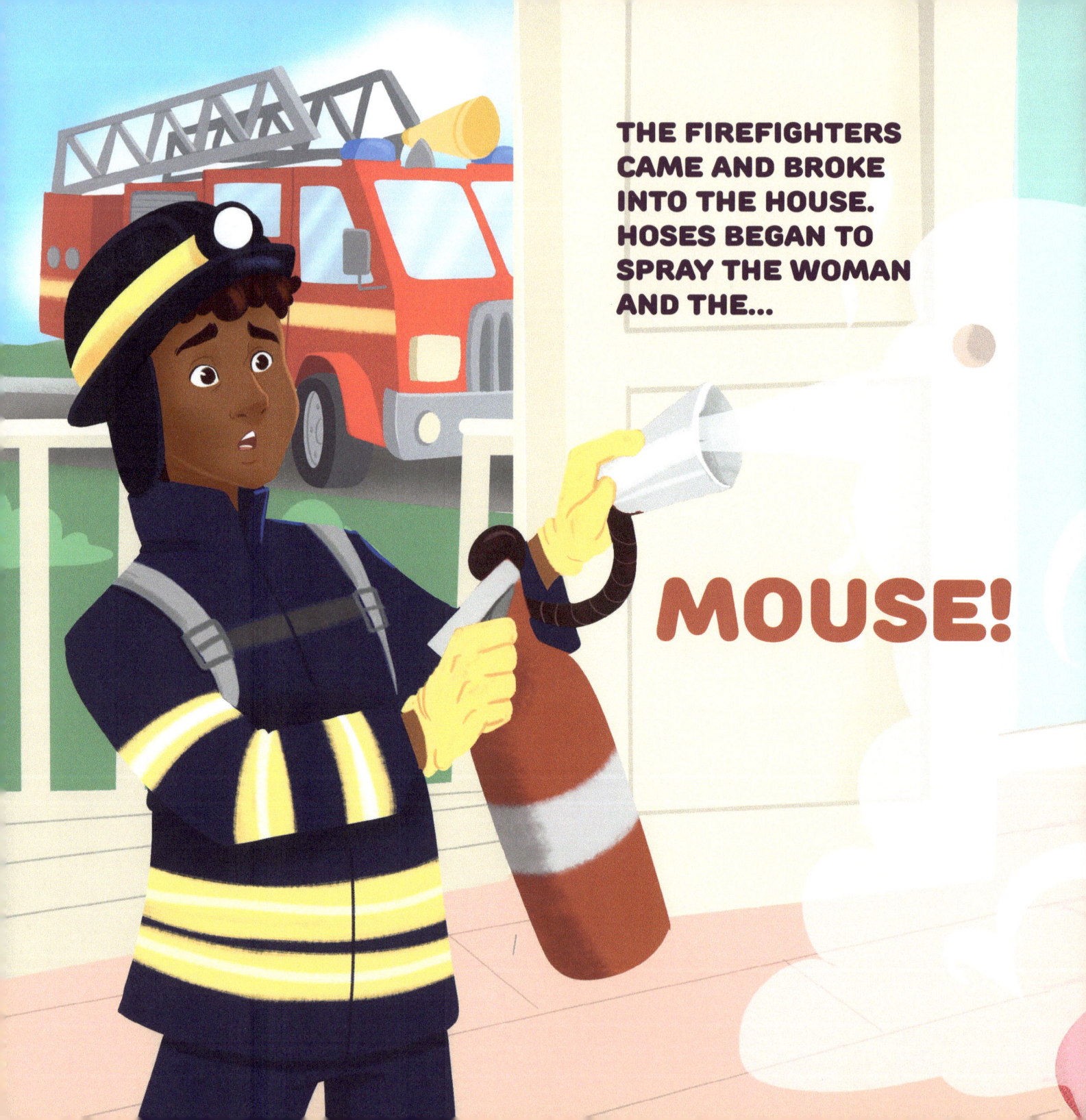

THE FIREFIGHTERS CAME AND BROKE INTO THE HOUSE. HOSES BEGAN TO SPRAY THE WOMAN AND THE...

MOUSE!

THE TWO SNAPPED OUT OF THEIR STARE. THE WOMAN SAW THE MOUSE AND CHUCKLED.

THE MOUSE LOOKED AT THE WOMAN AND GIGGLED. THEY BOTH LAUGHED UNTIL THEIR SIDES ACHED.

THEN THEY BEGAN COUGHING AND REALIZED THEY WERE IN DANGER.

DANGER!

SUDDENLY, THE WOMAN WANTED TO RESCUE THE...

MOUSE!

THEY HURRIED. SHE AND THE...

MOUSE!

SCURRIED OUT OF THE HOUSE
TO SAFETY.

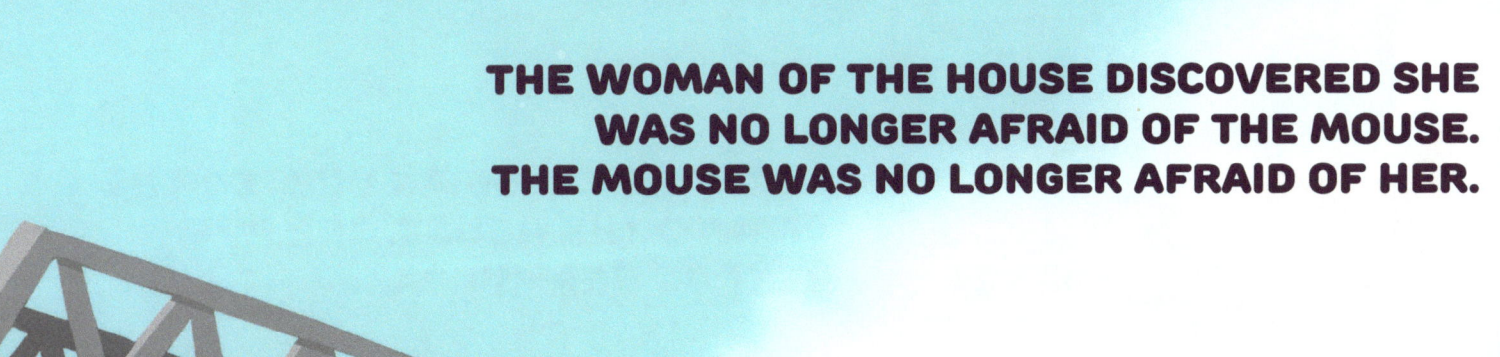

THE WOMAN OF THE HOUSE DISCOVERED SHE WAS NO LONGER AFRAID OF THE MOUSE. THE MOUSE WAS NO LONGER AFRAID OF HER.

WHEN IT WAS SAFE, THE WOMAN INVITED THE MOUSE BACK INTO THE HOUSE. SHE EVEN SHARED THE REST OF HER CUPCAKE WITH HIM.

THE END.

ABOUT THE AUTHOR

Carrie Hyatt is a devoted wife, mother, and grandmother. Her mission in writing children's stories is to create teachable moments that touch and bond readers and listeners through laughter and meaningful interaction. Her hobbies include writing, reading, and tending her water garden. Carrie loves spending time with her family. She and her husband run a chiropractic office in Oak Creek WI.

Visit www.carriehyatt.com, and discover the rest of the books in the Shout Fear Out series as well as other books by this author.
All of Carrie's books are available on Amazon.

www.ingramcontent.com/pod-product-compliance
Lightning Source LLC
Chambersburg PA
CBHW041558120626
46551CB00002B/247